Cackle, cackle, Mother Goose,
Have you any feathers loose?
Truly have I, pretty fellow,
Half enough to fill a pillow.
Here are quills, take one or two
And down to make a bed for you.

In loving memory of my mother

Barefoot Book, 124 Walcot Street, Bath, BA1 5BG

Introduction copyright © 2000 by Tessa Strickland. Illustrations copyright © 2000 by Clare Beaton
The moral right of Clare Beaton to be identified as the illustrator of this work has been asserted

This book was typeset in Celestia Antiqua 18 on 24 point. The illustrations were prepared in antique
fabrics and felt with braid, buttons, beads and assorted bric-a-brac. Graphic design by Design for
Publishing, London. Colour transparencies by Jonathan Fisher Photography, Bath. Colour separation
by Grafiscan, Verona. Printed and bound in Singapore by Tien Wah Press. This book has been printed
on 100% acid-free paper

ISBN 1 84148 072 X

British Cataloguing-in-Publication Data: a catalogue record
for this book is available from the British Library

3 5 7 9 8 6 4 2

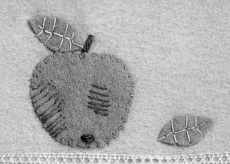

MOTHER GOOSE REMEMBERS

Clare Beaton

Barefoot Books
Celebrating Art and Story

www.barefootbooks.com

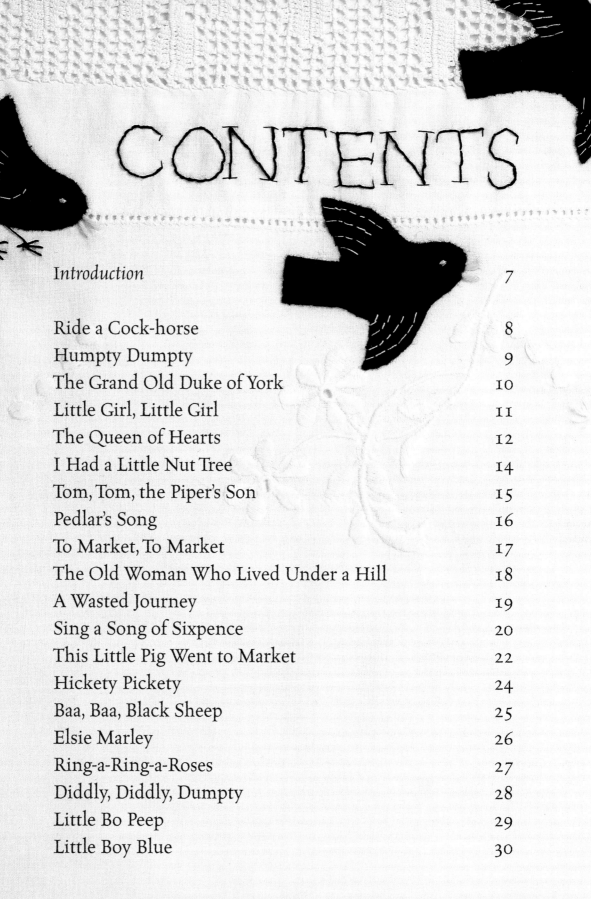

CONTENTS

INTRODUCTION

Mother Goose is a bird with a distinguished ancestry. As the carrier of the Hindu goddess Saraswati, who presides over the learning of language, music and the literary arts, the goose has been associated with the power of speech for centuries beyond telling. In the Neolithic temples of the north-east Mediterranean, excavated earlier this century by Marija Gimbutas, the head of a goose frequently appears on numerous carvings of goddesses. And with her white, snow-like plumage, this stately bird also has special connections with the north for peoples of both the Indo-European and Celtic traditions.

Mother Goose first flew onto the printed page in France in 1697 in Charles Perrault's book, *Contes de ma Mère l'Oye*. In English verse, she made her entrance with a collection published in London by John Newbery circa 1765. Since then, countless Mother Goose collections have appeared. Although their original meanings have almost been forgotten, many of her rhymes are steeped in symbolism and are closely connected to ancient agricultural festivals. They live on in all kinds of ways, some as plant lore, others as gently cautionary moral messages and others again as playful nonsense. No version of any rhyme can be regarded as exclusively 'correct', for their source has always been the ever-changing oral tradition, adapting itself according to the values, tastes and enthusiasms of each era.

In *Mother Goose Remembers*, Clare Beaton has selected her childhood favourites from Mother Goose's extensive repertoire, drawing on her fabulous collection of antique bric-a-brac to create a wonderful range of hand-sewn illustrations. A single feather from the plumage of Mother Goose floats on each scene, waiting to be spotted by youngsters and collected for a goose-down pillow at bedtime. May you and the children with whom you share this book have many hours of pleasure finding Mother Goose's feathers and sharing her timeless gifts.

Tessa Strickland
Publisher

RIDE A COCK-HORSE

Ride a cock-horse to Banbury Cross,
To see a fine lady upon a white horse;
With rings on her fingers and bells on her toes,
She shall have music wherever she goes.

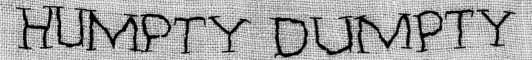

HUMPTY DUMPTY

Humpty Dumpty sat on a wall,
Humpty Dumpty had a great fall.
All the king's horses
And all the king's men
Couldn't put Humpty together again.

THE GRAND OLD DUKE OF YORK

Oh, the grand old Duke of York,
  He had ten thousand men,
He marched them up to the top of the hill
  And he marched them down again.
And when they were up, they were up,
  And when they were down, they were down,
And when they were only halfway up
  They were neither up nor down.

10

LITTLE GIRL, LITTLE GIRL

'Little girl, little girl, where have you been?'
'Gathering roses to give to the Queen.'
'Little girl, little girl, what did she give you?'
'She gave me a diamond as big as my shoe.'

11

THE QUEEN OF HEARTS

The Queen of Hearts
She made some tarts,
All on a summer's day;
The Knave of Hearts
He stole the tarts,
And took them clean away.

The King of Hearts
   Called for the tarts,
And beat the Knave full sore;
   The Knave of Hearts
   Brought back the tarts,
And vowed he'd steal no more.

I HAD A LITTLE NUT TREE

I had a little nut tree; nothing would it bear,
But a silver nutmeg and a golden pear.
The King of Spain's daughter came to visit me,
And all for the sake of my little nut tree.
I skipped over the water, I danced over the sea,
And all the birds in the air couldn't catch me.

14

TOM, TOM, THE PIPER'S SON

Tom, Tom, the piper's son,
Stole a pig and away did run.
The pig was eat, and Tom was beat,
And Tom went roaring down the street.

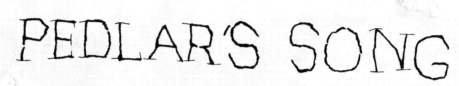

PEDLAR'S SONG

Smiling girls, rosy boys,
  Here – come buy my little toys.
Mighty men of gingerbread
  Crowd my stall with faces red;
And sugar maidens you behold
  Lie about them all in gold.

TO MARKET, TO MARKET

To market, to market, to buy a fat pig,
Home again, home again, jiggety jig.
To market, to market, to buy a fat hog,
Home again, home again, jiggety jog.

THE OLD WOMAN WHO LIVED UNDER A HILL

There was an old woman who lived under a hill;
And if she's not gone, she lives there still.
Baked apples she sells and gooseberry pies,
She's the old woman who never tells lies.

A WASTED JOURNEY

Hie to the market, Jenny came trot,
Spilt her buttermilk every drop;
Every drop and every dram,
Jenny came home with an empty can.

SING A SONG OF SIXPENCE

Sing a song of sixpence,
  A pocketful of rye;
Four-and-twenty blackbirds
  Baked in a pie!

When the pie was opened
  The birds began to sing;
Wasn't that a dainty dish
  To set before the king?

The king was in his counting house
  Counting out his money;
The queen was in the parlour
  Eating bread and honey;

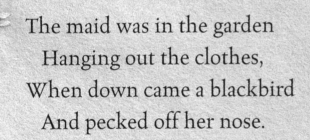

The maid was in the garden
  Hanging out the clothes,
When down came a blackbird
  And pecked off her nose.

She made such a commotion
  That little Jenny Wren
Flew down into the garden
  And put it on again.

THIS LITTLE PIG
WENT TO MARKET

This little piggy went to market;
This little piggy stayed at home;

22

This little piggy had roast beef;
This little piggy had none;

This little piggy cried,
'Wee, wee, wee!'
All the way home.

HICKETY PICKETY

Hickety pickety, my black hen,
She lays eggs for gentlemen;
Gentlemen come every day
To see what my black hen doth lay.
Sometimes nine and sometimes ten,
Hickety pickety, my black hen.

BAA,BAA,BLACK SHEEP

Baa, baa, black sheep, have you any wool?
Yes, sir! Yes, sir! Three bags full;
One for the master, one for the dame,
One for the little boy who lives down the lane.

ELSIE MARLEY

Elsie Marley's grown so fine
She won't get up to feed the swine,
But lies in bed till half past nine!
Lazy Elsie Marley.

RING-A-RING-A-ROSES

Ring-a-ring-a-roses,
A pocket full of posies,
Atishoo! Atishoo!
We all fall down.

Picking up the daisies,
Picking up the daisies,
Atishoo! Atishoo!
We all jump up.

DIDDLY, DIDDLY, DUMPTY

Diddly, diddly, dumpty,
The cat ran up the plum tree,
Give her a plum
And down she'll come,
Diddly, diddly, dumpty.

LITTLE BO PEEP

Little Bo Peep has lost her sheep,
And doesn't know where to find them.
Leave them alone, and they will come home,
Wagging their tails behind them.

LITTLE BOY BLUE

Little Boy Blue, come blow your horn,
The sheep's in the meadow, the cow's in the corn;
But where is the boy who looks after the sheep?
He's under a haycock, fast asleep.
Will you wake him? No, not I,
For if I do he's sure to cry.

30

31

PAT-A-CAKE, PAT-A-CAKE

Pat-a-cake, pat-a-cake, baker's man!
Bake me a cake as fast as you can;
Pat it and prick it and mark it with 'B'
And put it in the oven for baby and me.

LITTLE MISS MUFFET

Little Miss Muffet
Sat on a tuffet,
Eating her curds and whey;
There came a big spider
Who sat down beside her
And frightened Miss Muffet away.

33

HUSH-A-BYE

Hush-a-bye, baby, on the tree top!
When the wind blows the cradle will rock;
When the bough breaks the cradle will fall;
Down will come baby, cradle and all!

LITTLE JACK HORNER

Little Jack Horner
Sat in the corner
Eating his Christmas pie;
He put in his thumb
And pulled out a plum
And said, 'What a good boy am I!'

CURLY LOCKS, CURLY LOCKS

Curly Locks, Curly Locks, will you be mine?
You shan't wash the dishes, nor yet feed the swine;
But sit on a cushion and sew a fine seam
And you shall eat strawberries, sugar, and cream.

THREE BLIND MICE

Three blind mice! Three blind mice!
See how they run! See how they run!
They all ran after the farmer's wife,
Who cut off their tails with a carving knife.
Did you ever see such a thing in your life
As three blind mice?

THREE LITTLE KITTENS

Three little kittens lost their mittens,
And they began to cry,
'Oh, mother dear, we sadly fear
Our mittens we have lost!'

'What! Lost your mittens,
You naughty kittens!
Then you shall have no pie.'
'Meow, meow, meow!'

The three little kittens found their mittens,
  And they began to cry,
'Oh, mother dear, see here, see here,
  Our mittens we have found.'

'What! Found your mittens,
  You good little kittens,
Then you shall have some pie.'
  'Purr, purr, purr!'

39

LITTLE PUSSY

I like little Pussy,
  Her coat is so warm,
And if I don't hurt her,
  She'll do me no harm.

So I'll not pull her tail,
  Nor drive her away,
But Pussy and I
  Very gently will play.

POLLY PUT THE KETTLE ON

Polly put the kettle on,
Polly put the kettle on,
Polly put the kettle on,
We'll all have tea.

Sukie take it off again,
Sukie take it off again,
Sukie take it off again,
They've all gone away.

JACK SPRAT

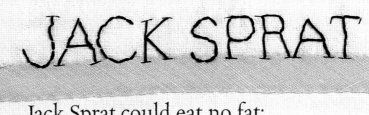

Jack Sprat could eat no fat;
His wife could eat no lean,
And so between them both, you see,
They licked the platter clean.

CUCKOO, CUCKOO, CHERRY TREE

Cuckoo, cuckoo, cherry tree,
Catch a bird and give it to me;
Let the tree be high or low,
Sunshine, wind, or rain, or snow.

43

THERE WAS A CROOKED MAN

There was a crooked man,
  Who walked a crooked mile;
He found a crooked sixpence
  Against a crooked stile.
He bought a crooked cat,
  Who caught a crooked mouse,
And they all lived together
  In a little crooked house.

45

SALLY GO ROUND THE SUN

Sally go round the sun,
Sally go round the moon,
Sally go round the chimney pots
On a Saturday afternoon.

A RASH STIPULATION

The daughter of the farrier
Could find no one to marry her,
  Because she said
  She would not wed
A man who could not carry her.

The foolish girl was wrong enough,
And had to wait quite long enough;
  For as she sat
  She grew so fat
That nobody was strong enough.

THE OLD WOMAN WHO
LIVED IN A SHOE

There was an old woman who lived in a shoe,
She had so many children she didn't know what to do;
She gave them some broth without any bread;
She then spanked them all soundly and put them to bed.

49

MARY, MARY, QUITE CONTRARY

Mary, Mary, quite contrary,
How does your garden grow?
With silver bells and cockle shells
And pretty maids all in a row.

APPLE HARVEST

Up in the green orchard, there is a green tree,
The finest of pippins that ever you see;
The apples are ripe and ready to fall,
And Richard and Robin shall gather 'em all.

LAVENDER'S BLUE

Lavender's blue, dilly dilly, lavender's green;
When I am king, dilly dilly, you shall be queen.

Who told you so, dilly dilly? Who told you so?
'Twas mine own heart, dilly dilly, that told me so.

Call up your men, dilly dilly, put them to work,
Some to the plough, dilly dilly, some to the fork.

Some to make hay, dilly dilly, some to reap corn,
While you and I, dilly dilly, keep the bed warm.

Roses are red, dilly dilly, violets are blue;
Because you love me, dilly dilly, I will love you.

Let the birds sing, dilly dilly, and the lambs play;
We shall stay safe, dilly dilly, out of harm's way.

Lavender's blue, dilly dilly, lavender's green;
When I am king, dilly dilly, you shall be queen.

GREY GOOSE AND GANDER

Grey goose and gander,
Waft your wings together,
And carry the good king's daughter
Over the one-strand river.

THERE WAS AN OLD WOMAN TOSSED UP IN A BASKET

There was an old woman tossed up in a basket
 Ninety-nine times as high as the moon;
 And what she did there, I couldn't but ask it,
 For in her hand she carried a broom.
 'Old woman, old woman, old woman,' said I,
 'What are you doing up there so high?'
 'I'm sweeping the cobwebs out of the sky
 And you can come with me, by and by.'

SNOW, SNOW FASTER

Snow, snow faster,
Ally-ally-blaster;
The old woman's plucking her geese,
Selling the feathers a penny a piece.

JACK, BE NIMBLE!

Jack, be nimble!
Jack, be quick!
Jack, jump over the candlestick!

HEY DIDDLE DIDDLE

Hey diddle diddle,
The cat and the fiddle,
The cow jumped over the moon;
The little dog laughed
To see such fun,
And the dish ran away with the spoon.

WEE WILLIE WINKIE

Wee Willie Winkie runs through the town,
Upstairs and downstairs in his night-gown,
Tapping at the window, crying through the lock,
'Are the children all in bed? It's past eight o'clock.'

HOW MANY MILES TO BABYLON?

How many miles to Babylon?
    Three score miles and ten.
Can I get there by candlelight?
    Yes, and back again.
If your heels are nimble and light,
You may get there by candlelight.

61

I SEE THE MOON

I see the moon,
And the moon sees me;
God bless the moon,
And God bless me.

Cackle, cackle, Mother Goose,
Thank you for your feathers loose.
'Twas my pleasure, sleepy head,
And now it's time to go to bed!

INDEX OF FIRST LINES

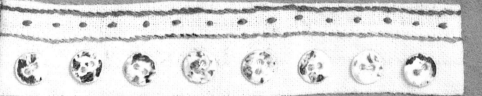

Barefoot Books
Celebrating Art and Story

At Barefoot Books, we celebrate art and story with books that open the hearts and minds of children from all walks of life, inspiring them to read deeper, search further, and explore their own creative gifts. Taking our inspiration from many different cultures, we focus on themes that encourage independence of spirit, enthusiasm for learning, and acceptance of other traditions. Thoughtfully prepared by writers, artists and storytellers from all over the world, our products combine the best of the present with the best of the past to educate our children as the caretakers of tomorrow.

www.barefootbooks.com